NEW

Zsuzsa Rakovszky

NEW LIFE

translated by
GEORGE SZIRTES

Oxford   New York
OXFORD UNIVERSITY PRESS
1994

Oxford University Press, Walton Street, Oxford OX2 6DP

Oxford New York Toronto
Delhi Bombay Calcutta Madras Karachi
Kuala Lumpur Singapore Hong Kong Tokyo
Nairobi Dar es Salaam Cape Town
Melbourne Auckland Madrid
and associated companies in
Berlin Ibadan

Oxford is a trade mark of Oxford University Press

First published in Oxford Poets
as an Oxford University Press paperback 1994

British Library Cataloguing in Publication Data
Data available

Library of Congress Cataloging in Publication Data
Rakovszky, Zsuzsa, 1950–
New life / Zsuzsa Rakovszky; translated by George Szirtes.
p.   cm.
A selection from 3 books of poems, originally in Hungarian.
I. Szirtes, George, 1948– . II. Title.
894'.51113—dc20   PH3321.R37N48   1994   93–14468
ISBN 0–19–283089–9

1 3 5 7 9 10 8 6 4 2

Typeset by J&L Composition Ltd
Printed in Hong Kong

CONTENTS

TRANSLATOR'S INTRODUCTION

IT IS unusual for one who is quite so young and who has published as relatively little as the Hungarian poet Zsuzsa Rakovszky, to be granted the status of a major-poet-in-waiting, nor is it always necessarily an unalloyed blessing: the notion of apostolic succession can engender too great a sense of responsibility in the writer and create professional jealousy among her eligible peers. Nevertheless when a voice as clear, as capable of speaking so passionately yet intelligently, is heard, people do tend to sit up and pay attention. As a result she has won all the major literary prizes available: the Graves Prize (donated by Robert Graves), the much coveted József Attila Prize, and the Déry Prize, twice. Her work has appeared in England, the United States, and Germany. At the time of writing her *Collected Poems* is in preparation in Hungary.

Zsuzsa Rakovszky was born in 1950 in the provincial town of Sopron, near the Austrian border, and studied English and Hungarian Literature at the Eötvös University in Budapest. She came to notice with her first book, *Prophecies and Deadlines* (1981), but her reputation was really made by the poems in her next, *One House Later*, published after an unusually long interval of six years. By the time her third book, *White-Black* appeared in 1991, Hungary and all the other countries of the region had changed irrevocably—or so one supposes.

It is partly the classical control, partly the brilliant clarity of her observation, that has attracted people to Rakovszky's work. While her poems tend to concentrate on what, at first sight, may appear to be intensely private experiences, with the themes of love, deceit, guilt, identity and personal loss uppermost, there is something in them that broadens their field of reference, a current of feeling encompassing a general and public sense of place and identity. The world of her poems is recognizably the world of her readers, a shifting urban landscape of noisy neighbours, malfunctioning television sets, shadows on landings, snatched meetings, and dying ideologies. To call her a Social Realist in the old sense would however be misleading. The realism she deals with is only one step from a kind of hallucination driven by desire; there is a process of disintegration evident in both object and setting. Essentially she is working in what remains of the tragic tradition, in circumstances where tragedy still makes sense if only because the stakes are relatively high. There is, in fact, a clear political element in her poems, but it is one in which politics is not so much a distinct issue as the stuff of life, a moral climate that conditions the most personal expectations. It is the world of Auden's 'The Fall of Rome' where anonymous clerks scribble 'I do not like my work' across official forms.

Most of the poems in the form of dramatic monologue and the longer more reflective poems come from the most recent book. The bulk of the translations however, including all the love poems, are from *One House Later*. It is interesting that, like a number of her prominent Hungarian contemporaries, she has translated copiously from English and American poets, and is very much at home in her second language. Temperamentally she draws a little on the confessional tradition of Sylvia Plath (readers might recognize a few echoes of both Plath and Emily Dickinson in some earlier poems), but her real affinity lies with Lowell, Jarrell and, for English readers, a poet like Carol Ann Duffy, though she is of a more intellectual cast of mind and presents a more fragile persona than the last.

The intellect is chiefly evident in the formal and narrative structure of her poems. The formal structure serves to discipline the strong waves of feeling that roll through her poetry: devices of rhyme, strict metre, syllabics and stanzaic form allow her occasionally to dispense with punctuation altogether. I have rendered these in English to the best of my ability, firmly believing in their centrality. They are not icing on the cake: the cake would simply not exist without them. The narrative structures can be equally complex, sometimes elaborating a detail, at other times cutting sharply across to a new perception. This is a matter of pace and tone. Rakovszky's is racy, fast, flittering but precise: despite the elaborate forms, she is essentially informal. The lines are rarely end-stopped but run across each other in a colloquial manner. This raciness prevents the poems from sinking under their intellectual and emotional freight. Nothing—not words, not phrases, not even metres—mean precisely the same in one language as they do in another. Nevertheless poems can be translated, providing they remain poems. Where I suspected there was an English equivalent that meant for us what the original meant for Hungarian readers, I have looked for it. I have tried to balance the form against the lexicon, maintaining as much of both as I could believe in. The poems in this book are translations, not 'imitations' in the Lowellian sense. Rakovszky sounds natural in Hungarian: I have tried to make her sound so in English. To put it more precisely, I would like her to sound in English as she sounds to me in Hungarian. This self-appointed task, while demanding, was always rewarding, always a delight.

GEORGE SZIRTES

AVART ÉGETTEK

Avart égettek. Dőlt a must szaga,
buzgott a kátrány.
Bogáncson ellenfény holdudvara,
tépett szivárvány.

Az utca erdő—mélyebb ősz fele
lejtett az este.
A szélső ház—a hánytorgó zene
majd szétvetette.

Még egyszer ezt, csak ezt, és mást sosem
többé: leszállnék
az őszi alvilágba, jobb kezem
kezedben, árnyék—

('They Were Burning Dead Leaves', see p. 16)

THE HARMONIC SERIES

for Tamás Hermann

'The harmonic series is divergent.'

We forgave him this opinion for a while.
After all, everyone's different and each
to his own, et cetera. At most we hoped
that in due course, with the benefit of experience,
he'd see things differently. Gently but firmly we drew
his attention to the fact that life, after all,
is more complex than *this*. We referred to
the difficult economic situation, the unfavourable
weather, and reminded him that such inflexibility
can come to no good. We tried to appeal to his
tender feelings. We told him: think of your
widowed mother—or of ours at least, our rheumatism,
our childhood traumas, our hard times and
difficult upbringing. Then we told him he knew
nothing of real life, that the overwhelming
majority of people did not think like this.
And we reminded him—with no ill feeling of course—that
even he wasn't perfect, and that he
had committed a few errors in his time.
And if he hadn't—well, he would. His gross obduracy
naturally succeeded in annoying even us
in the end, but we must emphasize, we only used words
to influence him. That is to say we warned him first in
    person,
then in writing: we fined him a hundred forints
and sentenced him to be beheaded: we confiscated
his shopping vouchers, his season ticket, his standing orders;
we tore off his right ear first and then the left;
we placed him on the index; dropped him down a well,
removed him, racked him . . . in other words
we used these and other methods of persuasion on him.
Pain failed: for all our good intentions it was like
flogging a dead horse; the
harmonic series continues as it was, divergent.

CONNECTIONS

In general, things may be divided
into two categories: one of which I'm guilty,
one of which I'm not. We may safely ignore
the second.

I understand it is my hair which has blocked
the sink again. I'm told it was me
who brought influenza home. It is for me
they had to stay up till midnight, to moil and toil, to sell
the little silver box, and the spangled nightdress
done up in gift wrapping. All right. I'm incorrigible,
not in what I do but what I am. It's better though, I know,
not to err on the other side, or else
there could be no punishment: behind the numbered door
on the flaking white bedside table, phials
of medicine, half-full glasses of orange juice, and the rest:
wreaths whose roses are turning brown, a tattered
dark ribbon, soaked letters of gold—such consequences
must naturally follow. Could I have caused
the earthquake in Athens? The eclipse
of the moon? It is my wicked influence
that spreads and swells the winestain on the table.

The accusing voice of a little girl with a drooping
mouth; a freckled hand always screwing up something:
a paper handkerchief, the newspaper, the fringes of
an invisible tablecloth. Irresolute little button eyes
accuse, accuse—silly round hats
in old pictures, a handbag like
a tiny mushroom, the victorious baroque pleats
of an ankle-length summer frock before
a bed of irises or a jetting fountain;
the glistening collarbone above the
narrow shoulder straps—surely I must possess immense
powers of destruction.
Before you realise it, something is squeezed out,
a price has to be paid, you are caught in the net
of transgressions, counter-transgressions . . .

I dream sunlight, a room, the clinking of dishes—meanwhile I
    know
there's someone behind the wall, in a smokeless blazing room . . .
and the door's unlocked: but it's not me, not me, not me—

BEACH

She stands,
    black waves reaching to her thigh
(a faint negative stocking), above it she's
walled within the rushing body of wind

Round her the silent water, luminous sand in tiny
frozen wrinkles, sharp shadowed
footprints—then another stripe
of water: runnels spilt over chipped
marble into the bowl of the fountain.

. . . Textile patterns across light-blotched skin
like flora of an alien planet: white branches
against blood-red sky, flowers that fit in a palm;
or dark-monochrome torsos whose sharp edges
restrain a volatile longing for lushness
(fevered thoughts in the mind of the air).

. . . Limbs dawn in dark
water, waves break in cages of light
where green arms and palms hover—a ring
flashes blindly.

. . . In them soul
is an infection, a foreign fire: a foul weight
on flesh delightedly burgeoning in light. Eyes crackle
on the live fabric of shoreline: tide vacillates
between water and cabins, draws a ring about
departing tradesmen. It is as if
they were balancing the water, trying
to calm some inner storm within it—
Lost time flashes in empty mirrors, threatens
long-postponed encounters.

. . . Your nervous lashes droop
as you lean on your elbow; dust clings

4

to the down on your arm—above you
pine needles of darkest silver—

wind rises, carries the sand, the whole shore is in flight,
mats, blankets, gowns beat against the sky or take to
    the water
you too are swirling there with the rest of them,
a tiny weightless leaf. The slumped bronze disc of the sun
drowns in clouds of sand.

SZOZOPOL

A blinding white leaps from the postcard view:
from its noon cathedral sun issues
articles of fire. The town
collapses in light as in a stream of blown
froth, or sinks like rotting fruit, heartsore,
to the bitter stone at its core.

Steep courtyard cobbles burn our soles: a branch
of the fig tree bends under the avalanche
of a shower, branding the dark wall
with a fiery mirror. Noon burns like alcohol,
a hand fishing for truth in hot primordial soup,
fries, hisses and breaks up.

Hovering between house and beach the sun
drains off like water in a bath, goes down
while orbiting its hub in vacant rings.
Metal strewn across glass: reality ablaze.
Not opinions or delusions, faint rumblings
of theological disputes, or holy days.

Holidays, time in inverted commas: you come in
to a cool house: taste of red wine, salt on skin,
the voluptuousness of dry lightning, you seem
to inhabit a borrowed body, never the epic theme
of fraud, disappointment, failure, family,
but the flight of a swing in hollow ecstasy.

Nothing to be done while this eternal present
falls about our ears: only the moment
with its isolated sparks of brief askesis.
A point, never a line, never essence,
never opinions or delusions, nothing happens
to us or ever will, nothing but this.

EPISODE

It's hardly worthwhile noting down which door
leads where—in any case I won't be tapping
my way round the angles of this dark corridor
again, seeking a doorknob, wary of waking
who knows who with a creaky floorboard. Why
take especial notice of a stranger's flat anyway?

In the dim glow of the bathroom mirror
I make out cans of sprays, a double row
of toothmugs, and as in the flash of a camera,
myself in agitated outline. Despite this show
of belonging, I'm out of my element,
a foreign body lodged in an alien event,

no more. But even if the postulated soul
is missing, every gesture of the mock
sacrament enacted on that preliminary roll
of tartan—variations on a common stock
of ideas, but so many and so individual—
in other words the whole neckbreaking ritual

works with such a fluent passion that the cursed
heroine can remain in perpetual mute arrest
even if it's the hundredth time and not the first
when, between deep blue sea and prompter's box,
she shakes her terrified incredulous locks
to stare fixedly at the hand across her breast.

ADULTERERS

Such brilliant devices! . . . We might seize
state secrets at shorter notice with less
ingenuity: tearful conspiracies

in filthy cafés, snatched phonecalls . . . Not to mention
varieties of setting: back seats, a bare lawn
—the underview of a branch—in borrowed accommodation

with lamps in bottles and embroidered cushions
. . . Or right here, between accustomed walls, crushing
each other—clumsy burglars—in brief conflagration,

leaving no fingerprints (we hope) . . . And time remains
strangely flexible: a windy alien season
sneaks between its ribs—until it heals again,

emergency exists firmly sealed and we strain at the lock
in increasing panic as our heating goes on the blink,
and, having consumed the air, we start to choke.

SNAPSHOT

August balcony evening six
it grows darker I am happy
and unhappy Horizontal lines
freeze in mid-flight Perspective
draws me downward I'm happy
and unhappy The shadow of
the terrace opposite has crept
across the street and begins
to slide up our wall One by one
it extinguishes the green glow
of plants in stoneware pots on
the neighbour's balcony I'm happy
and unhappy and don't let don't
anything happen It might break
the water inside me whose tense and
balanced surface no longer wishes
to mirror anything but unblemished
space I am happy and unhappy
am and am not happy and am and . . .

9

ONE HOUSE LATER

Here not just yet, here never more:
light slinks about the house, sighs through each room,
through each little corner: now refrigerator,
now sink or side or bathtub bloom
white in the half-light, and I open and close doors
or wash up glasses, in this place no more
in that place not yet, but for the time being
all of these things: broken-down washing-machine
in corner, window-sill darkened
with polyp-cacti, holiday postcard the width of my hand
pinned to mirror on wash-stand;
I'll re-inhabit these in memory. What was firm,
conclusive, occupied space, will henceforth be
absorbed as life in a living body, lodged within time.
Someone's pouring water before the house: for
a brief instant before grey darkens to a patch
of darker grey, a shadow line, there's a splash,
an explosion, a whole galaxy speeding away.
    As the branch shifts
outside, the linoleum floor of the verandah
ignites and goes out. Here never more, but
other times, elsewhere, a slow wave falls
tossing me to consciousness, to new walls,
new cracks, eyes waking to a new crop
of images in a new order, spinning to the top
of the whirlpool which isn't anywhere,
so one time I should be here, another there.

WILD NIGHT, WILD NIGHT

Wild Nights—Wild Nights!
Were I with thee
       Emily Dickinson

Morning, not night—tightfisted
in all things: our eyes
are watching the clock even in bed,
we scramble into clothes, but though we rise

alert, our senses locating routine,
agenda and form, circumstance
dictates to us—our times together have been
a matter of chance,

the odd exceptional moment . . . tempting providence
to count on such again.
I could take malicious glee in the past tense,
in missed opportunities when

I changed the sheets, or set out drinks for two.
Devising a solution to bluff
us both into one room requires a compromise ever new,
a greenness ever coming into leaf.

To speak of the debt due to passion would
be as ridiculous as one of those 'chic'
old hats decorated with a bowl of fruit
or a stuffed peacock,

enough to raise a snigger. To say OK,
let's give in and separate,
is such a cliché it seems almost new. But who'd pay
the price of it:

our two bodies hungering for each other,
redeemed by consciences in apple-pie
order? And the absence, the loss, would that be no bother?
It'd sting us like a gadfly.

11

To fabricate a lifestyle from the sheer necessity
of striking a pose
would take greater fanaticism, greater vanity
than we can impose.

So we get by in our moral no-man's-land,
with every reason
to make one harsh decision, or to let things stand,
each according to season.

SILVER AGE

Undergrowth in the light-speckled coniferous forest:
between thick trunks a clump of silver trembles.
Light zigzags among pines slicing ground into segments
needles of compost sprawl across bare earth.

Cobwebbed raspberry bushes, frosted berries, fields
of rape behind the walnuts, now just glimmering clods
turning to steam. Further back, two long buildings,
granaries. Muscat grapes shimmer further up the hill,

dark of chestnut trees which signify temptation.
Infidelity is simple: even if I'd been happy,
why should I remain so? Heavy, overripe, happiness
drops from my heart: I do not insist on it.

It is as well the rain has started: a bleaker, busier
serious season has arrived. Now one may scamper, run
for the bus, panic, grasp at things. Only the weensiest
scruple remains: the diminution of my own significance.

SONG

Your price was far too high
now I wouldn't take it free
hunger consumes itself
if you simply let it be

Is your cupboard bare of honey
is it sitting on the shelf
either way starvation
slowly devours itself

So what if time provides
the meal we might have had
time might have been spent better
though times just now are bad

Replete with what I lacked
I've no desire left now
So much I wanted it then
but not anymore nohow

CHANGE

Yesterday, sunbathing in
as yet uncut grass Eyes
flooded, yellowish-white, green
stalks not yet on the rise,

but so many greens and so
many bristling hills combed
back by gusts of wind which blow
across so many domed

brows in all directions, just
playing, appearing at
intersections, to draw us
into their games and what

hope that was that bled away
Meeker more reclusive
light shows end-of-the holiday
scenes misty-impassive

drifting—but I see them
from beneath a bubble
of glass, which renders them
at once intangible

THEY WERE BURNING DEAD LEAVES

They were burning dead leaves. Must oozed with scent,
    tar bubbled and blew.
The moonlight glow behind the thistle bent
    like a torn rainbow.

The street was a forest, night slid into the heart
    of deepest autumn.
A guilty music blew the house apart,
    with its fife and drum.

To have this again, just this, just the once more:
    I would sink below
autumnal earth and place my right hand in your
    hand like a shadow.

MORNING

Translucent dish of the morning:
a neutral effervescence, not
yet interfering with the ground
colour of sensation, a

swarm of images is milling
at the huge window, sky with branch,
wind with grass, shadows of curtains,
ever new and improvised

when you come: my attention thins
to a seething uncontrolled point,
and oozes out of the focal
centre becoming background.

EVENING

Outside what strikes through russet
brown as red and white is a
shadow play, curtains glowing
in pools on the banister
Carpet mossed with light, woven
tightly across the pillow
Only glass in icy blue
shards arrests its steady flow
Shadowgrids burn triangles
into sliced trapezia
Books glimmer in their lost spines
The hideous wallpaper
fades My room is cut into
two equally dark halves by
a wall of thin embers From
a dark armchair I dip my
toes into it they catch light
when I pull back they go out
A thin fluid hand frisks our
cool bed now sliding about
the sheets drawing the relief
of our bodies from its folds
unwrapping a memento
of the sunk morning which holds
my thighs whose shadows still grip
the shanks of your shadow hip

INSOMNIA

The sun has ground down; but walls are throbbing
with activity: the chandelier radiates
wild spokes of light, pleats and wrinkles of glass
projected across the ceiling: insects throng
a central halo, wreathed about a single point,
their vast shadows billow through zones of light.

Windowpane: a charcoal room swims through grey water.
Light's dim double sways, a reduced incandescence,
flat black forms float through the mist like mourners
of something left over, long dead. Light irritates,
sheathing my flesh in nylon, sheer, sticky with
perspiration; it melts and dazzles like boiled sweets.

The dial's luminous: I daren't go to sleep.
A dead woman lurks in the precincts of my dream:
she is cowering in her usual place on the divan,
or preparing to leave: she fiddles with her
knitted skirt which sizzles and clings to her stocking.
She paints her mouth, applies a pencil to her brow,

searches for her book, or for knitting needles in
a basket. I avoid her glance: she mustn't know . . .
by dawn she will have become a piece of paper tumbled
by the wind, an empty dress. She comes time and again
whenever I drift into broken sleep, from which
time and again I'm woken by lightning: her blinding
jagged profile, leaning against a phosphor-bright sky.

SUMMER SOLSTICE

August already, and the sky's a dull
    mother-of-pearl dispensing sunstroke.
I watch exhausted branches of sumach poke
    through holes in a tarred roof.
A woman sunbathing on a pale beachside
    lawn twists a towel into a turban,
grows dizzy, examines herself in a pocket
    mirror, sucking in her cheeks.

The melon's flesh is green glass, apricot
    swells with blood. The streets
are hot candyfloss, everything is see-through,
    melting. Ice cream dribbles
cold pearls sizzle on perspiring skin
    your shirt is sticky.

The sounds of a TV film rise from the well
    of a dark courtyard, all windows open.
I wake startled, my curtains undrawn,
    someone has forgotten to switch off
the grey sky whose blank humming screen
    glares down at me.
Last year's dead sit on the usual chair
    just beyond my field of vision.
In my dream a pale foot struggles upward
    through muddy earth.

Gladiolus explodes in slow motion, unwinding
    from foot to crown:
it survives a few days, while the red or yellow
    flame rises to its peak.
At night a white light glows behind my closed
    lids: a comet appears on
the horizon, spinning and shaking,
    a huge bird of light, brooding, calling me 'daughter'.

Chandeliers are slowly being turned
        above us: Leo glows and shifts
into Virgo, henceforth everything will be different.
Whatever is completed drops through the sieve, whatever
        is ripe comes to an end—
or doesn't end, things are just about to begin,
        keep calm, keep calm, keep calm.

WAITING-ROOM

This friendly room is like a well-meant
conspiracy or a hushed-up scandal,
with its slender vases, wide somnolent

chairs, and a pile of last year's glossy mags
on the crocheted tablecloth. Between dark
silhouettes of houseplants a few frayed rags

of sky are visible above the narrow street.
Our only clue is the picture of a faint
nude on the opposite wall, stretching before velvet

curtains—how enigmatic!—and how innocently
she hints at the bed within, at rubber gloves
and at the point where high technology

meets startled flesh. We watch each other, disciplined
and fully dressed: parading anxieties
like toy balloons that drift in a low wind.

Do I really want this? Am I free to want something else?
Or only this, these bittersweet crumbs,
clichés of tenderness, possessiveness?

these wars of religion for ever bickering over
idols of flesh and blood? We are always using
each other's towels and toothbrushes, their

truths strangle my truths, at night I hear them
at arm's length, breathing to rhythms
alien to mine, while the flotsam and jetsam

of the world accumulates in me, heavy as salt,
I'm becoming opaque—do I want to feel
so much, in such a haphazard fashion, and all

for nothing? Or should I remain, a sheet of virgin glass, a frozen possibility, behind which time catches fire, my time—later, later again.

NOON

Not half an hour since,
your skin on my bare skin
the foam of love making
still nestling in folds of flesh
two feet fall apart one left
one right, the sun crashes,
from blunt heat wings whirr
their sussurus a red pulse
invades my womb as if
in a half-sleep I had conceived
by two fathers a pair of twins
sisters one blonde one dark:
one of whom throbs and aches
while the other glows and is not.

PAINTING BOOK

above scarlet roofs the
blue sky small nothing clouds
I might have painted them
in childhood an almost
unused palette almost
unused world precisely
as white as blue under just
such roofs as if beginning
as if something were starting
chide me now, don't look dumbly
away in case I should feel
cheated by time, be harsh
don't let me hope again or
rush madly round in circles
I am tired don't let me

RAINING

raining raining it started
this morning summer gone out
a match dipped in water
it will fall now a long time
mad summer cools slows down
grows sluggish grey spills
across blue yellow red
brilliant now streaming down
windows damp wind behind
a great whale flounders in
the gutter its colours
oil and mud raining why
should we go out and do
things do nothing nothing
flop on the bed together your
arm under my neck for
a long time since nothing
can happen for a long time
no going out now for
a long time it will rain
now for a long time it
will rain for a long time

SONNET

'If you don't love me now, . . . ' I shook with cold
throughout the night. Morning is much the same.
Two simultaneous cramps—while one takes hold
of bowels and hips, the other nips my brain.
Top and bottom halves balance out. I'm sick
but don't throw up, and stumble to the shops
to indulge in one mad prophylactic
spree on childhood consolations: lollipops,
almonds, a bag of sweets, the same old stuff.
Is this my lot? All baby-talk and pet
names? For ever to turn and turn about:
now parent, now child, now Adam, now Yvette?
I might be cured. If one could be warned off . . .
But would it work? . . . *Your pain will seek you out.**

* a line from Attila József (1905–37)

FROM THE DUTCH SCHOOL

Groceries and herring on a table, or
a deck of cards scattered round dimpled glass.
In a chilly blue-green dusk, huge wagons ford
a stream, bearing an inferior class
of cabbage. Cellar stairs grow intimate,
winking under rain. A hand lifts a torch:
its faint effulgence picks away at night
unpeeling ivy and a corbelled porch.
By isolating them, the picture frame
draws out the sheer assertiveness of things,
a simultaneity in which herrings
cabbages and lit torches all proclaim
their *are* and *were*. But beyond such ebb and flow
lies time's third option: *not-here-not-I*. *No-go*.

LOVE

This predator—could this be love? This flood
of feeling oblivious to all but its own
concerns, for whom the world must be scaled down,
reduced to a walk-on part, a moral cud.

The swivelling of greedy eyes which see
nothing but one thing: saying no, it is not I,
but something driving me, you must see why
I can't do anything, *it* governs me,

Not I *it*. And whether music or scent
or touch are the triggers, gradations remain
constant and contiguous, a logical chain
of values with a common referent:

which says no rules exist except exception,
that *needs must when* . . . that neither fidelity
nor gratitude count—and that mere humanity
is unable to face the competition

of what simply happens; going on to assert
the anatomical truth, proved under the knife,
that all the fundamental energies of life
love Being and care nothing for Desert.

Death at the hands of conscience turns to thirst,
desire for revenge, blame laid at the door
of precisely those most prized before,
the best neatly become the worst:

you'll see what furies I've reserved for you
if you should bar my way, or dare to damp
the fires that light me like a lamp,
and glow within my cells the whole day through.

So rigged and mined a terrain it is
joy drags me to, such dangerous rays bombard
my soul, goodness and gratitude almost blow me apart,
I neither feel nor acknowledge my inanities,

although once I am sober, I'm so sickened by
my unsuspected cruelty, it disgusts me more
than nail-biting, a habit I deplore,
but one that will stay with me until I die.

ICE

Ice to the horizon patchwork ice grey-green.
Distance on distance the quality of dream
white-crested moon-ice a reddish Chinese
drawing in ink behind reeds behind a frieze
of ice mountains bristling an autumn scene
under a winter one when did it last babble its mean-
ingless bluetalk or ceaselessly reason with stones
on the beach, that myopic element sparkling–darkling
dilating on the spot a fat woman in a bathing
costume was still smearing oil on herself on a thin
lawn among abandoned swings and stands in
almost-summer light and now instead this grey–
green sheet of moon-ice which won't say
I'm yours possess me the sun-and-milk smell
of summer bodies while summer clarities of purpose shuffle
off leaving a grey enticing waste with which there's
    nothing to
be done. We sat on the shore then looking out, the two
of us, our plurality lending the spectacle
a brighter more indulgent significance. Gentler
spirits of autumn freeze behind the winter imagery.
Stubbled moon-mountains reddish reeds and leaden sky
despite which some outrageous sense of freedom
tells us that whatever it is that must come
is coming (it'll come anyway) and since it is coming
you were we were and I can lose nothing.

FESTIVAL

We are sipping a coke on the Italianate terrace,
metallic music in the square below us
blossoms as we watch daylight colours freeze
on bright walls aspicked in shadows;
yellow houses turn nightmarish. Beneath,
the square is spinning as its blood flows
away. Chemist and post office flatten
like stage sets in a geometric pattern,

and round the observation tower the fashion plate
saying *You are invited* . . . is overshadowed
by a surreal advert for whisky: *Der Tag geht,*
its lilac fringed by pale gold while below
the patriotic and sentimental music brays
and rattles through its paces, strutting through
familiarities that each of us will know,
from gruff military airs to the Merry Widow.

Summer trade supplants the local traffic.
Slowly the square fills up like a tray:
Austrian women in dirndls blend with thick
matrons and pink–blue tides of autumn babies,
but we sport our broad expressions and graphic
gestures to proclaim that whatever way
we were screwed up, this is where it happened,
here, long ago, we bit the rotten apple,

and like some complex psychological disorder
it burgeoned in us all, individually,
so now it no longer matters that this sordid
state of compliance has settled permanently
in our souls, and that which was once forbidden
is simply handed over to us, free,
and we wear our dread as a badge of profundity
the way neurotic Viennese women wore sex last century.

It was 'on these shores' that I—but what of that?
Our histories and multifarious values
emerge vaguely from a value-free twilight,
but like sunlight stored in walls that ooze
their warmth at night, this too demands I put
the residue to some specific use
not merely pinch what I can here and there.
It pulses with life like people in the square,

and things that *were* offer up their reasons
for all that *is*. Waves of scorched weed
tremble by the bus-stop, height of season.
Market shimmers by car-park, one bleeds
into the other. Bunched darkness flows across the lawn
below. Syringa bushes. Things appear fragmented,
dissolve to events—solid walls are shot through
with liquid light, nouns with verbs: *to be* is *to do*.

The machine, wound down, still hums under glass:
as piles of *things that were* grew vast
they filed and compiled and assembled a whole class
of useless fortuitous parts which at last
became everything that is the case—within its mass
traces of a mould remain, the impression of a cast
slowly boiled over, one which could not see out
the age and time's quick deliberate drought,

so slid across into some final slot of time,
like decapitated figures of Juno and Zeus,
illuminated tombs housing Roman officers of dim
significance in the basement of the Fabritius
Museum of Monuments, or two floors up, begrimed
portraits of chimneysweeps and oculists. Continuous
loosening of continuities, chains of causation:
the new is unfit for life, remaining stillborn.

The past still dribbles on in dribs and drabs—but what
will happen when even this is gone? When we go
more wraithlike still, more battered, or strut
on an ever barer stage which offers nothing, no
union of chimneysweepers, no street parties, not
even streetsigns, merely a maquette in the afterglow
of a living sky. Like a visiting company
of exhausted players, who summon a certain energy

for the last scene, all top-hats and brio, while
floodlights dip the square in silver and gold
pools that catch at our ankles in the aisle,
I find myself in the crowd, hunched and rolled
along with them down a side street where they tail
away, breaking into fragments, while the cold
space they once occupied with human warmth is
filled with night, lilac and seamless.

BLACK AND WHITE

They threw the live rat on the fire: it hissed,
a rat-shaped shadow among orange flames,
later delicate bones, a rodent frame
in a museum behind rippling glass,
finally less than that. Redundant kittens
are drowned and tipped out with the litter
to be discovered like soaked squares
of fur, cigarette ash, old onion skins.
Meanwhile the sky is blue, the sun still shines.
the grass is green and this is all impossible.
One after another, ranks of pale
apparently dead twigs break into bud,
the sun dips its needle into shards
of green glass in last years yellow grass, noon
pours across weedy allotments heralding
summer, ten million cabbage whites drift on
the wind, while above the sprawling lawn
spin sylph-white molecules of dandelion
seeds. Everything is fine the way it is,
believes the eye. But in the mind there flows
an endless simultaneous debate,
pro and contra talking at once, to sort
these images (but who is to speak for whom?)
A lab assistant, all ice and bone, weighs
rats against dandelions. I must sort through
all the arguments, the black and white ways
of logic and blackmail, then cast my vote:
a big yes or big no to the whole lot.

COUPLES

The wrist-watch crushed beneath the heel in a blind fury
    or with methodical calm. The reply
in ever more filthy terms of abuse, the frozen caricature
    reflected in the mirror of the eye.

The curt fortnightly exchange, the dumb automatic
    routine among boxes of Lapsang Souchong.
The terrible rage beneath the mask, the cinematic
    gestures in slow motion like a film gone wrong.

The beer, the wine, the half-empty bottle of tablets
    carefully timed, the very last cheap
argument on the seventh floor, the dash for the gallery
    where some do, some do not, make the leap.

The blithe, the well-mannered ones, the kindly ones, at a
    concert,
    in the theatre, at rail or bus terminals.
The madness ticks in the shared bed and waits to blast a
    sheet
    of flame about buses, trains, hotels.

The old yet new world set to explode into light and leaves,
    at the very beginning. The rose,
the dawn, the dew, the gratitude, the blind force that
    deceives
        in trembling hope or so the poem goes.

PAPER BOATS

That time and circumstance are a foolproof
barrier . . . don't you believe that stuff!
Psychologically though . . . ? Perhaps some truth
in that. At six, say, you practically fall off
the bridge with the cranky rail, leaning out
to see whether the paper boat you launched
three steps away on the far side has made it
safely through. And say it manages to ride
the darkly shadowed water, a branch may catch
it or the frothing miniature waterfall clutch
it to its white belly and drag it under—
but say it survives that too, and has scampered,
accelerating, practically keeling over,
to the black throat, the very threshold
of the arch of that black corridor where suds
of water pass beneath the ground, and with raised prow
moves under grass, stone, and earth although
its waterproof tinfoil has unwound, towards
the open waters, out of the stink of sewers
and into another town, where if you were
to arrive in your coat with its mangy fur
collar, no one would mock you, saying, 'Who wears
such things nowadays?'; it wouldn't matter
if you took sugar in your tea, nor would you
have to quake in your boots while lying to
a squint-eyed schoolmarm with the face of a bloater
knowing she knows, only in nightmares.
Purity and goodness must exist somewhere,
or what's a bleak life for? Possibilities
remain: you may launch your personal qualities
as often as you like on genuine seas:
the more experience you have of a slut
the easier to imagine an angel, though
you can never quite decide precisely what
to call her: memory? or hope? It's hard to know.

AS

Like descendants of those abandoned by
a lost expedition, a group surviving
on raw meat, turned eskimos by necessity
in a world of polar snow that hurts the eye
and an unquenchable, copper-coloured, infuriating
sun, who in order to assuage the seemingly eternal
tedium of the white night, invent the decimal
system, gunpowder or the alphabet,
between the dusk of oppression and the dusk of habit
which is different, the tremendous self-evident
truths leap to attention in a festoon
of light, and that for us is still a privilege, most
privilege when most obvious; since later at best
they ooze pale beams like streetlamps lit at noon.

OLD WOMEN OF MY CHILDHOOD

What else was there? The cocktail cabinet with pillar
base and marble top of raw-liver colour.
Cups thinning in light to a grey mist, a few
back numbers of a magazine called *New
Age*, silhouettes of greyhounds in an oval frame,
a souvenir glass, engraved with the name
of a German town. Their mode of being was curious:
imagine a cuckoo clock or ten-piece dinner service
salvaged for one's sole convenience from a wreck
and cast on a deserted beach among the bladderwrack
twixt goats and palm trees. Why furnish a room
with two tall facing mirrors? To reflect the gloom
of an unlit damp apartment, with neither kids nor maid?
Who'd use silver spoons for gruel, or provide
a pair of sugar tongs for a grain of rationed
sugar? What hope obliged them to preserve old-fashioned
gowns in the purgatory of the laundry chest?
Did they imagine themselves elegantly dressed
on promenades in fashionable parks, wearing one of those?
When did they realize that earnest suitors would not propose
to me in country residences while under the spell
of my dazzling rendition of *Für Elise*? Who can tell
what delusions they laboured under, the poor fools,
firmly convinced that fate would observe minimal rules
of etiquette, or how they contrived to maintain
their innocent beliefs. One might explain
away a dose of sickness or penury . . . but this?
Alice, grey-haired, meanders in a mist
of manners, still wearing her lacquered shoes;
having no clock-sense she's likely to confuse
the times of day; her dreams are like stiff dough.
(Better, perhaps, a dream world that you know
than a half-cock universe beyond control.)
Meanwhile the clocks chime on and hours unroll
as if time still existed and was somehow theirs
bringing a green–white froth of roseblight to squares
never referred to by new official names,
or twisting snow into apparitional white flames

to crown a bronze lion's monumental mane or shroud
the transmitting tower that sends time-signals out.
For one last time the broken blinds will clatter down,
patches on walls grow expansive, blotches of brown
skin on hands wear through, cigarette-paper-thin,
and watering eyes sink ever deeper in
a hutch of soft crushed bags. What else is there?
Only an over-exposed photograph, a white spectre
or candleflame in the foreground: outside, it might
be a winter evening, inside: electric light,
a festive tablecloth's sharp crease intrudes
into the picture and a fogged mirror broods
in circles. In clots of shadows which probably
dominate the background one might be able to see
among barely discernible patches, a faint outline
sufficient (with a little imagination) to define
a chin, shoulder or an unknown hand whose grey
boundaries too are finally washed away.

AS IF

Before the peeling yellowish façade
of the sanatorium, set in the glade
of a frozen park, sheets of steam smother
a green oblong of medicinal water.
Shadows swirl in the mist, spinning now right
now left as they approach in crooked flight:
if the shadows are rooks they twist and flap
landing in the leaf-mould; if leaves, they tap
down slimy steps and stay there, smoothing away
what edges remain. Each gust clatters a dry
host of dark spirits into furious motion.
Some find the pool and drown in a green version
of the beyond, glowing beneath the dome
of sizzling glass like perfect polychrome
corpses. Shadowless, harbourless, on the wing,
they're neither active, nor mutable nor living,
but merely exist. It is as if a warm
transparent layer of eternity found form
in the hinterland between two words. As if
you could somehow preserve an afterlife
of last year's heat and snow. As if there were
a half-way house to which one might repair
to rest intact. As if time could be pumped
from a place, with no past, and nothing to come,
but a night of glass and steel and burning lamps:
the lamps still lit, and long removed in time
from what they are; and so, by changing tense,
one might be able to keep them in some sense.

TRANSLUCENT OBJECTS

Greenwich Flea Market

Only the sewing machine is missing. Free
association according to the laws
of chance assembles umbrellas, golf-clubs, ski-
boots, under the free sky where instead of sauce
a thin grey mass of clouds creeps tremulously,

darkening like thunder over cruets and jugs
(Bosch monsters with half an ear or lower
lip on a limbless torso). Should wind shrug
them aside, five ranks of polished brass door-
handles are waiting to advance in their frogged

uniforms, and trays of rings, stones upward,
shimmer like roe at a dragon hatchery.
Who wore this butterfly brooch? These buttoned
gloves? At what ball? How many years of study
went into this monograph on swordfish offered

to 'my patient spouse'? Bloody Mary's bowl
and Anne Boleyn's sampler were intended for
the public gaze, they don't make us feel
like intruders or voyeurs. But this poor
cat-shaped vase, and this one-eyed doll,

this ice-blue, sky-blue, piece of glassware
in which God neglected to plant concave fruit,
collected on a dissecting table of noon air
and stripped of their forgiving layers, their suit
of sensibility, still seem to be aware

of the bright feeling of being at square one,
where everything might yet turn out OK—
under the Christmas tree, as a freshly un-
wrapped wedding present or an ancient birthday
gift, redolent of childhood, youth and home.

Cut free of its own past each joins that mess
of organs sprawling on the surgical plate
of history. Our cold eyes weigh the price
of strips of broken skin and sagging breasts, too late
for the selective myopia of tenderness.

DECLINE AND FALL

At last they will disappear, finally just go,
those cinemas and cigarettes named after terms
derived from military history or constitutional law.
The waterworks, machine-tool factories, firms
producing matchboxes that advise you to pursue
a prudent lifestyle, they will vanish too.
Local branches of the catering industry,
chipped teacups, tubular plastic barstools made for short
legs, flat drinks in bottles whose labels sport
sundiscs and oranges as if the real sun had bleached
them both, tables with marble effects and sticky
tops. They'll survive a while, persist like rime
in the coldest microclimate, in random patches,
but when they do eventually go it won't be time
but earth which swallows them, they will flake off
and soak away: anniversaries, occasions of formal
mourning, ersatz occasions that pass for normal:
Mother's Day, Women's Day, Children's Day, Sports Day,
each with its posters scrubbed, peeling away
to reveal a flowering branch or dove, or a block of
numbers pasted across a girl's virginal face,
(as if atoning for a Playboy playmate's vast
overthrusting bunny bosom pressing against lace),
all these will fade away, as will the products
of the Totalitarian-Classical, filthy terminals
and waiting rooms, provincial culture halls
with monstrous frescoes and mosaics docked
of odd teeth, showing humanity gathered
in full-throated choirs, celebrating harvests,
or the manufacture of ball-bearings, breasts
heaving in joy at the redemption of leisure
by culture. Not everything has weathered
so well: where are the experiments with white mice
or ferro-concrete? Burst like a balloon,
a thousand pieces exploding in one vast bloom,
or stretching, shrivelling, curling in long flames
resembling, if in nothing else but this,
a contemporary Rome or Babylon's nemesis.

44

My mass-produced mirror, my pot of jelloid facecream,
my little brown jugs, will not grace a museum,
provide educational outings for family Sundays,
nor will my remains be preserved in an airtight case
or my colour-rinsed curls and protruding eyes
be twisted into a sheath—my speaking likeness
will not be hung on the wall to oversee the moral
welfare of a new generation; indeed, of the wall,
a prefab component of my industrial highrise,
of that whole moon-grey incubator where each block
rots faster than the inner city's overblown baroque,
not a jot will remain. A few turn-of-the-century
public buildings, like slices of elephantine
wedding cake, blackened and growing green,
might yet survive, but their bills designed
for the propogation of an ornamental diction
and their six-foot streamers will have declined
and faded, their threadbare carpets rotted
to an ultimate state of dereliction,
and dehydrating yellow leaves of potted
palms perished in civic halls where council
employees, women in business suits, fill
forms, harangue, register marriages,
and rooms where we presented ourselves, signed up
for birth, death or divorce perhaps survive
preserved in memory's indifferent syrup
only while we who lived them are ourselves alive.

DESERTED GIRL

Once again the post,
goes unchecked: although something might well be lost
in the shallow darkness of that oblong slit—
it's not just a piece of dawn-dull tin, not just . . .

It need not arrive
until tomorrow: that slim provocative
vertical white edge might be a circular,
or hospital appointment. Should I survive

the day only to
find what I had hoped might be a curlicue
of handwriting is an official label
to remind me that my books are overdue . . .

Meanwhile, the static
hours with their usual dumb typewriter-tick
go on repeatedly stabbing at the x,
a wallpaper pattern, pale and anaemic . . .

Hours, time emptied out
and flattened: oh, if only my time were stout
and substantial; if only my thin body
were caressed and swollen, but I've gone without

such pleasures before.
Last night I watched a scribbled sky above more
aerials than I could count, a cooling wash
of neon, the feathered clouds combed out to raw

fringes, sulphurous
yellow, smoke blue, steel grey; pure childhood colours,
the after-tonsils gift of a paintbox, lined
with little cakes of pigment in two tin rows.

Clear before water
flooded them, labelled rims of carmine, ochre,
red and blue were set round a peacock design.
And there was something you could fold out, not a

book, but almost one—
in which a scarlet post office crackled on
blue ground, where pink roses spattered yellow walls
and red seats glowed in a provincial station . . .

Whatever I saw
looked back at me, wholly absorbed me: I knew
no pain or wrong, no guilt, no gleam of desire:
salt in water, water in salt, washed through

and no love followed
in its wake, glinting and sharp, like a swallowed
razor: the fire glimmered outside, not in me,
it wasn't I but the whole world which billowed

in its flames. Now what
has come between us? My body? What has cut
that stream of joy? Has the flood frozen or dried in me?
Do I exist at all? Or all too comprehensively?

ADDICT

What's the alternative? What else is there, tell me?
The stuff others use? I see them on buses,
in the street—their faces anxious and flustered,—
and none of them looks as though she were exactly

delirious with joy simply because she's not on
the needle, because she contrives to live
in the blissful knowledge that for five
days in seven she can lug cheese, batter

away at a typewriter or carry a full bedpan.
There are rewards of course: once home
in my cosy flat, in my one and a half rooms,
I could pot geraniums on my balcony,

smooth the ruffles in my carpet, reap
the fruit of my labours. Well one could do worse.
There are real pleasures, spring, summer, the birds
twittering in the branches, cheep, cheep . . .

And love, of course. The many-splendoured thing.
You know the scene. You're lying on the bed,
staring straight up, nothing in your head
but the bloody phone which doesn't want to ring . . .

Half-past seven, eight o'clock—the day
stretches out interminably. Whatever
you look at turns caustic, burns like a fever.
One day I told myself: no more. OK,

but assume that he loves me, perhaps even
marries me. What happens then? Pretty soon
we're down to doing it once in a blue moon;
I'm no longer a woman but a cross between

the Virgin Mary and an old biddy with the shakes.
Tell me I'm wrong. It was the same at home.
Why should I put up with it? Must I come
to this? Did I ask to be born, for heaven's sake?

Perhaps I did apply to join the club. But when
did I accept rules which mean you suffer some
sixty, seventy years, and have in that time
the odd enjoyable minute now and then?

So what if I cheat at times, I have no choice.
The game is safe now: the points mount as I score
and win. Cut the cards a dozen times or more,
or flash the bright lights, I still turn up the ace.

And what have I lost? A graceful old age? When
I gently pat the pool, my turbanned tortoise-
head held above the water like some precious
ornament so my make-up shouldn't run,

doing my dutiful fifty lengths per day,
so that my friends may remark, that although I'm
eighty I don't look a day over seventy. Next time
I'm bedbound, dunking my teeth on a tin tray,

fed through a shiny tube from a plastic bag,
while my skin is bluish green around the veins,
and I burn and shrink in fires without flames,
with my nurse well out of earshot, the old hag . . .

No problem really—my genes and everything
I've done survives me. That should cheer you up
knowing that somehow you don't come to a stop,
though I've read the universe is collapsing

into itself, or is it expanding? Much
the same thing really. It's hard to accept that
not just me, but earth, sky, light, sound, must go zap,
leaving a thin or dense nothing, a big zilch.

49

Even time will go. But time does not exist
in any case. I know. I saw. As the sun
rose and touched the dripping tap in the kitchen,
it shone like a bird-headed goddess, a crisp

little peardrop dangling from her beak, until,
its patience worn thin by its weight, it gained length
and narrowed and began its feeble descent:
an eternity passed as it hovered, still

before that snap, and I watched and felt something
click into place and I knew it was the world:
that God is joy. In drip and tap it's him, pearled
and perfect, and if you don't know this you know nothing.

NEW LIFE

For keeps this time? Why not? The flat, it's true,
is crammed to the hilt with others' history,
but what if it is? Theirs will not be too

different from yours. Some potted greenery
brought in for winter . . . three, four months swim by
and you don't even notice the scenery:

crash-helmet on the wardrobe, the pleated sky
of a deep-blue fan pinned out against the wall
like a dead bat, on which two pochards fly

skeetering towards the shelf . . . Puffy, dropsical,
the doorpost is swollen about rusted locks
(flesh round a wedding ring). A faint pall

of dust on the lamp whose little brain box
reflects the light, fire's pallid baby sister.
Is this a kind of vision, or simply how it looks?

*

A couple of years, and you don't even think of moving.
Or you might, but know it's just not on. Your friend,
D, will not move either, but will still be striving

with vibrant Dostoevsky's soul, and spend
the next five hundred years hunched over the screen
of his word processor; nor will there be an end

of J, the musician, trailing his scores between
the ground floor and the third, not to mention the Pekes
inherited from his girlfriend, trembling, obscene,

up greasy wooden stairs. A's lousy TV freaks
her out, with its constant humming, heads and busts
of terrorists or commentators with El Greco physiques,

grey skulls aflame in interstellar gusts.
True, she might, if the neighbours got her riled,
eventually fix the doorbell, but the mower rusts

in the shed, and our famous 'lawn' grows wild
in winter, every little weed in furious sprout,
as if the bio-clock were running a self-styled

republic, and had surreptitiously winkled-out
an immaculate display of bleeding hearts,
a hard sell of bright shrubs in shameless rout,

crab apple, Japonica, like common tarts
to strut against a swirling February mist,
the anaemic catkins' less effective arts.

Those straggling off-white hordes in the park insist
on being sea-gulls, stiff, triangular,
and not the soft white geese your eyes first promised,

winged spools, awkward in flight. How spectacular
the sun is when it shines . . . it casts a fleeting halo
of backlight about trees and grass which are

ideas of greenness but real ideas! And oh
how its thoughtful fingers search my rough tweed coat
for tiny bits of fluff that cling like snow . . .

*

Two, three years, there's no doubt now: unfazed
by sheer excess, by eighteen kinds of mustard,
I've found my favourite cereal, appraised

the various brands of bathsalts, and adjusted
to being nun or nautch-girl, jewel or jade,
eternally fidgeting in Monday's busted

après-festive pallor, or busily parade
my maddening superiority like a sailor who's
been to Hades. I've earned my accolade

by pitting dark experience against the ingénue's
blank innocence. The bellows driving the high
clouds of my vanity might wear out or refuse

to work, but there'd be air enough for them to hover by
till I grew tired and the ever less spectacular
changes of season, or the rain-blurred years' spry

progress offered me a part more in the vernacular:
teacher or housewife, or—why ever not?—
a leader in the struggle for gay rights or the Popular

Front for the Liberation of Animals, with a pot
of paint at the ready, and a razor in my hand
to slash a bourgeois fur: this could be my lot

if a plain existence were denied to me. (And
why should it? Seagulls, fire and catkins
are plain enough, you won't miss them.) To aband-

on your life is a matter of sloughing skins:
the check-out girl at the grocer's, an Albanian
on the game, tries to recall her origins

as a Friesian fisherman, or a lady in Japan
with a little white dog at her heels . . . Always
there is something . . . Something beyond the span

of time or space, from which their combined rays
are simply deflected, as from bulletproof glass . . .
some tiny dense trapped particle, something one pays

like an unreturnable deposit, like a compass
pointing beyond endless dark . . . a needle in a haystack . . .
Is there such a thing? *Well, is there? Well? I pass.*

OXFORD POETS

Fleur Adcock
Moniza Alvi
Kamau Brathwaite
Joseph Brodsky
Basil Bunting
Daniela Crăsnaru
W. H. Davies
Michael Donaghy
Keith Douglas
D. J. Enright
Roy Fisher
Ivor Gurney
David Harsent
Gwen Harwood
Anthony Hecht
Zbigniew Herbert
Thomas Kinsella
Brad Leithauser
Derek Mahon
Jamie McKendrick

Sean O'Brien
Peter Porter
Craig Raine
Zsuzsa Rakovszky
Henry Reed
Christopher Reid
Stephen Romer
Carole Satyamurti
Peter Scupham
Jo Shapcott
Penelope Shuttle
Anne Stevenson
George Szirtes
Grete Tartler
Edward Thomas
Charles Tomlinson
Marina Tsvetaeva
Chris Wallace-Crabbe
Hugo Williams